Seeing Jesus

Four Portraits *of an* Unlikely Savior

ADRIEL SANCHEZ

C·C

Seeing Jesus: Four Portraits
of an Unlikely Savior

By Adriel Sanchez

© 2021 Core Christianity
13230 Evening Creek Drive South
Suite 220-222
San Diego, CA 92128

All rights reserved. No part of this book may be
reproduced or transmitted in any form or by any means,
electronic or mechanical, including photocopying,
recording, or by any information storage and retrieval system,
without permission in writing from the publisher.

Design and Creative Direction by Metaleap Creative

Printed in the United States of America

First Printing —January 2020

CONTENTS

05 INTRODUCTION
Why This Booklet?

09 CHAPTER ONE
The Bridegroom Who Pursues You

19 CHAPTER TWO
The Priest Who Deals with Death

33 CHAPTER THREE
The Lord of Creation

45 CHAPTER FOUR
The Zealous Redeemer

INTRODUCTION

Why This Booklet?

THE MORE I READ THE BIBLE, the more I'm amazed by it. When I first started reading the Scriptures, I didn't know just how spectacular they are. Sure, I accepted them as God's inspired Word, and I knew they were filled with wisdom for today. It took me a long time, however, before I discovered the internal consistency of the Bible—that all of Scripture, from Genesis to Revelation, is one story. *The story of redemption.* This one story fixes our eyes on Jesus, whether it's through types and shadows in the Old Testament (for example, think of the temple with its sacrificial system), or the revelation of the Son of God in the New Testament. All of the Bible fixes our eyes on Jesus, and his apostles followed this example (1 Cor. 2:2). It seems to me that good Christian books and ministries are those that do the same. They help us to know Jesus better, highlighting what we often tend to miss.

Sadly, missing Jesus is a very real possibility for each one of us, *especially those of us who have grown most familiar with him.* We're reminded of this in one of the most tragic stories in all of the Gospels:

> [Jesus] went away from there and came to his hometown, and his disciples followed him. And on the Sabbath he began to teach in the synagogue, and many who heard him were astonished, saying, "Where did this man get these things? What is the wisdom given to him? How are such mighty works done by his hands? Is not this the carpenter, the son of Mary and brother of James and Joses and Judas and Simon? And are not his sisters here with us?" And they took offense at him. And Jesus said

to them, "A prophet is not without honor, except in his hometown and among his relatives and in his own household." And he could do no mighty work there, except that he laid his hands on a few sick people and healed them. And he marveled because of their unbelief. (Mark 6:1–6)[1]

Did you catch that? The people who thought they knew Jesus the best had completely missed him. *Isn't he just the son of a carpenter? We've watched him grow up!* If it happened then, it can happen now. We can have a false familiarity with Jesus that actually blinds us to his true identity. Many people today accept Jesus as a great moral leader, or a spiritual guru, *but think he wasn't perfect*. He's one way to God for some people. He was the carpenter's kid, *not God incarnate*. When this "hometown" Jesus (who is really nothing more than an idol) is shattered by the biblical Jesus, often people get offended. Even *you* might get offended.

In the church, we can grow familiar with a hometown kind of Jesus. He's a savior we've made in our own image who has come to deliver us from our greatest fears. He came to lead us into the green pastures of health and happiness, all the while overlooking the sins we still cling to. It's not just those outside of the church who can have a hard time seeing Jesus clearly; even among those who confess Christ, there's a lot of Jesus missing. If that wasn't the case, I don't think Paul would have prayed like this for the church in Ephesus,

> [May] the God of our Lord Jesus Christ, the Father of glory . . . give you the Spirit of wisdom and of revelation in the knowledge of him, *having the eyes of your hearts enlightened*, that you may know what is the hope to which he has called you, what are the riches of his glorious inheritance in the saints, and what is the immeasurable greatness of his power toward us who believe, according to the

---

[1] All Scripture verses in this study are taken from The Holy Bible, English Standard Version® (ESV®). Copyright © 2001 by Crossway, a publishing ministry of Good News Publishers. All rights reserved.

working of his great might that he worked in Christ when he raised him from the dead and seated him at his right hand in the heavenly places. (Eph. 1:17–20; italics added)

We need the help of the Holy Spirit to reveal to us the true beauty and love of Jesus, lest we settle for a figment of our own imagination. One of the ways the Spirit does this is through God's Word. As we open the Scriptures, and God opens our hearts, we come to know the great hope that Christ has purchased for us through his death and resurrection. The goal of this short booklet is to help you see Jesus better by taking a closer look at some passages of Scripture you may have skipped over before. We want you to see Jesus as the *bridegroom* who pursues you, the *priest* who deals with death, the *Lord* who controls the universe, and the *zealous redeemer* who purifies your heart. Only when you grasp who Jesus truly is can you benefit from a personal relationship with him! As Paul prayed, may the eyes of *your* heart be enlightened so that through the Scriptures you might see Jesus clearly.

Prior to each chapter, we encourage you to *pray*—asking God to help you see Jesus clearly through the text—and then *read* the passage being considered. After you've worked through the passage, read the chapter and think through it. We've provided some questions at the end of each chapter for reflection. This is a great exercise for you to do alone or with a group of friends.

CHAPTER ONE | *John 4:1–26*

The Bridegroom Who Pursues You

AS I MENTIONED IN THE INTRODUCTION, the unity of the Bible is spectacular. Sixty-six books written over hundreds of years with a central theme: Jesus. Of course, we see other themes throughout the Bible, but even these aren't unrelated to Christ's identity. Take, for example, the biblical theme of the bridegroom. As we all know, a bridegroom is the man who is about to be married. We typically just call him *the groom*. And as we also know, there can't be a groom without a bride.

In the Old Testament, God called Israel his bride. Their "wedding ceremony" is described in Exodus 24, when God entered into a special relationship with his people known as a covenant. This solemn ceremony bound God together with Israel in a unique way, as Israel pledged herself to obey God, and the promise was sealed in blood (Exod. 24:7–8).

Later in the Bible, the prophets would refer to God's spiritual marriage with Israel, because of what took place on Mount Sinai (Jer. 2:1; Eze. 16:8). In the Bible, Israel's sin is often depicted as spiritual adultery, precisely because of her marriage relationship with the Lord (Hos. 1:2–3; Eze. 16:32). Israel longed for the day when that broken relationship would be restored. This restoration wouldn't happen as the result of Israel's faithfulness or worthiness, as she had broken her covenant promise. It would happen only because of God's loving pursuit of his sinful bride (Hos. 2:15–20).

This marital tension between God and his people is the context in which Jesus came to earth. Remarkably, one of the things we're meant to see about Jesus in the Gospels (especially John's Gospel) is that he is the bridegroom who pursues his bride. How God refers to himself under the old covenant is how Jesus reveals himself in the new covenant: in the incarnation, Jesus is the bridegroom who pursues his spouse.

Now who exactly is Jesus pursuing? Who would you pursue? If you're single, where do you hope to meet your potential spouse? Or if you're married, where did you meet your husband or wife? Was it a blind date? Did you meet at a club or in the church?

When I was in college, there was a local frozen yogurt place called the Yogurt Mill that was located just a few miles nearby. I attended a small Christian liberal arts school, and the joke on campus was that if a guy took a girl to the Yogurt Mill, he was destined to marry her. It was totally fine to go to the Yogurt Mill on your own or with a group of friends, but if you were meeting someone at the Yogurt Mill *alone*, that would raise eyebrows as everyone knew the Yogurt Mill is where you meet your future spouse!

Although it's not a mill nor does it sell yogurt, there is a similar meeting place in the Old Testament—the place where a man of marriageable age meets a woman of marriageable age and becomes betrothed. Here are some Scripture references to jog your memory:

» In Genesis 24, Isaac's wife, Rebekah, is discovered at a well.

» In Genesis 29, Jacob meets his wife, Rachel, at a well.

» In Exodus 2, Moses meets his wife, Zipporah, at a well.

Scholars have noted some of the factors that tie these stories together. In each of them, there is a man traveling to a foreign land who meets a woman at a well and becomes betrothed. Now think about how this colors John 4 when Jesus—the bridegroom—intentionally traveled to a foreign place (Samaria) and met a woman *at a well*. No wonder this raised the eyebrows of the disciples. It should raise our eyebrows too! Not just because Jesus met a woman at a well, but because of the specific woman he intentionally sought out.

Here's another question: If you're single (or when you were single) what kinds of qualities are you looking for in the person you hope to spend the rest of your life with? We assume you want them to be attractive. Maybe funny. Maybe intellectual. Someone you can have a good conversation with. Someone who comes from a good family, who you can bring home to your parents, and who doesn't have a lot of extra baggage to lug into the relationship (that's important, right?).

When Jesus seeks out this woman at the well, we get the sense she's not the kind of young woman a respectful Jewish man—a rabbi no less!— would pursue for several reasons. First, she's from Samaria (4:7), and the Jews in Jesus' day didn't associate with Samaritans. This is clear enough from the response of the woman to Jesus in verse 9, "How is it that you, a Jew, ask for a drink from me, a woman of Samaria? (For Jews have no dealings with Samaritans)." From the get-go, this is an odd matchup indeed.

If you're wondering why there was tension between the Jews and Samaritans, it goes back a long way to an unpleasant time in history. In 722 BC, when the Northern Kingdom of Israel was conquered by Assyria, it was repopulated by pagan nations that brought their idolatrous practices into the land, and who simultaneously sought to worship Yahweh along with those other "gods." What they ended up with was a mixture of Jews who remained in the Northern Kingdom and probably intermarried with these new pagan neighbors who settled in the land, *adopting some of their pagan practices*. This is known as syncretism—an ungodly blending of religious practices that would have been repugnant to zealous Jews.

The Samaritan rejected the Jerusalem temple, and instead installed their own temple at a place called Mount Gerizim. Interestingly, at one point this woman tries to get into a religious debate with Jesus about the right place to worship, saying, "Our fathers worshiped on this mountain, but you say that in Jerusalem is the place where people ought to worship" (John 4:20). The text reveals to us that she and Jesus aren't even on the same page when it comes to religion!

So, this woman doesn't come from the right family (she's a Samaritan), and she doesn't understand the basics about how God wants to be worshipped. Those two facts alone make her an extremely unlikely candidate for marriage with a religious Jew. But there's more that we find out about her. This woman has some serious skeletons in her closet. She's had a troubled past and a hard life.

> Jesus said to her, "Go, call your husband, and come here." The woman answered him, "I have no husband." Jesus said to her, "You are right in saying, 'I have no husband'; for you have had five husbands, and the one you now have is not your husband. What you have said is true." (John 4:16–18)

Now, in our day, it isn't uncommon for people to get divorced and remarried. Sadly, our society doesn't regard marriage as highly as God does. But even by our standards, five husbands is a lot! In those days, it would have been jaw-dropping. It would have raised a lot of questions too. Perhaps some of her husbands had died, but the most likely answer is that they had all left her. And right now, she's living with a man who is not her husband, which would have added to the scandal.

Five times divorced, now living with some random guy—it's no wonder she's at the well in the middle of the day. We're told it was the sixth hour, the afternoon. In the arid desert, this is not the time anyone wants to go out and draw water. Usually, they do that in the morning, when it's still cool outside. Not the Samaritan woman. Many commentators suspect she's there in the heat of the day, alone, because she doesn't want anyone to see her. She's an outcast, living with shame. In her mind, finding true love—one who will never leave her or forsake her—is probably not an option anymore. She's given up looking, but not Jesus. He hasn't given up on her. This woman is a picture of the bride of Christ, the church, baggage and all!

In the well betrothal scenes of the Old Testament, sometimes we see a man bringing gifts for his potential bride. Jesus, too, has a gift for this woman. "If you knew the gift of God," he says, "and who it is that is saying to you, 'Give me a drink,' you would have asked him, and he would have given you living water'" (v. 10). Professor Brant Pitre of Notre Dame University notes that "living water" was sometimes associated with the custom of a Jewish bride undergoing a ritual bath before her wedding. The idea reminds us of Ephesians 5:25-26 where Paul writes, "Husbands, love your wives, as Christ loved the church and gave himself up for her, that he might sanctify her, having cleansed her by the washing of water with the word." Jesus washes his bride for the wedding, and he himself is the source of the life-giving water. Jesus said, "I am the bread of life, whoever comes to me shall not hunger, and whoever believes in me shall never thirst" (John 6:37). He reiterates this same point just one chapter later: "If anyone thirsts, let him come to me and drink!" (John 7:37).

Now, just in case you're still doubting this whole bridegroom connection with Jesus and the woman at the well, consider the fact that one chapter earlier, John the Baptist said,

> "I am not the Christ, but I have been sent before him. The one who has the bride is the bridegroom. The friend of the bridegroom, who stands and hears him, rejoices greatly at the bridegroom's voice. Therefore this joy of mine is now complete. He must increase, but I must decrease." (John 3:28–30)

In the context of John the Baptist's words, John's disciples were concerned that Jesus' ministry was growing and that everyone was going to Jesus (not John!) to be baptized. John's response was, "Hey, that's great news. *He's the bridegroom!*" In other words, Jesus came to gather his bride, the straying people of God, and in the very next chapter *Jesus seeks out the woman at the well*. He offers her himself, the living water.

When and how did Jesus give this woman the living water? According to Professor Pitre, we find out at the end of the Gospel when the apostle John mentions something about Jesus' crucifixion that we don't find in any of the other Gospel accounts. In 19:34, he writes, "But one of the soldiers pierced his side with a spear, and at once there came out blood and water." Talk about living water! In the Old Testament, God's people were forbidden from eating food with blood because the "life is in the blood" (Lev. 17:11). Here we have the lifeblood-water flowing from his pierced side, from his heart. It is the blood of Jesus that washes sinners, that gives us life, making us a part of the bride of Christ.

This, however, isn't the first time a bride was created from the side of someone in Scripture, is it? Think back to Genesis 2, when God put Adam to sleep and from his side created Eve. At the end of John's Gospel, we see the second Adam on the cross, and from the blood that flowed from his side, a new bride, the church, was formed. And who does Jesus pursue to be in the church, his bride? People who came from the wrong families, who didn't worship God the right way, who have all sorts of baggage, who have been rejected and neglected. Dear friend, Jesus pursues *you*, and through his shed blood, he makes you a part of his bride, the church.

You know what we see in Jesus here in John 4? We see that no matter who you are, or how hard your life has been; no matter how many times you've been rejected, or have failed, Jesus still pursues you as he did this woman. It wasn't her merit or righteousness. It wasn't the pure life she had led that brought Jesus to her that day. It was *his heart of love that would soon be pierced so that she might be washed*. Jesus pursues sinners, and that should fill us with a humble love for him.

Here's another thing we see about Jesus here: he wants *intimacy with his people*. The God of the Bible isn't distant or aloof. He's not a heavenly judge eagerly waiting to crush us with his cosmic hammer because of our sins. He's the bridegroom who pursues us, even though we have sinned. The spousal relationship is personal, marked by tender care, affection, and closeness. God wants that kind of relationship with you. This isn't about simply having the right answers to a theological exam; it's about *seeing Jesus clearly* so that you can know him *personally*. Do you know him like that? As the one who pursues you despite your failures and who wants intimacy with you? That's the kind of bridegroom he is.

DISCUSSION QUESTIONS

1. What's the significance of the fact that, throughout the Old Testament, God was the bridegroom of Israel, and then when Jesus showed up in the New Testament, he was identified as the bridegroom?

2. What does this story reveal to us about the kind of people Jesus pursues? Do you think our churches reflect this Jesus-like pursuit of sinners, or are we afraid to pursue sinners like Jesus did?

3. Read John 4:39–42. Do these verses give you any insight into the mission of the bride of Christ in the world today?

4. We can sometimes pit knowing Jesus against having a personal relationship with Jesus. It's clear from this text that God wants both: intimacy with his people and proper worship (note especially 4:24). How can you balance these two things (the head and the heart)? Do you believe you have a good balance of these in your own life?

CHAPTER TWO | *Mark 5:21–43*

The Priest Who Deals With Death

ONE OF THE MOST DIFFICULT PASTORAL SITUATIONS I've ever encountered came a few months before I was officially ordained as a pastor. It was one of those situations they talk about in seminary but you can really never fully prepare for. I received a request to go to Children's Hospital in San Diego to visit a family I had never met who had just lost their four-year-old daughter.

Typically, hospitals have chaplains on site for this kind of thing. For whatever reason, the chaplain was not in that day, and a nurse at the hospital happened to be a member of the church I was interning at during that time. When she heard the family wanted someone to come and pray with them, she called the church office to see if any of the pastors were available. Due to the short notice, I was the one who ended up taking the call. I remember praying for the family the entire ride to the hospital. I was asking God for wisdom, having no clue about what to say to the family. "Lord, help me have the words for them, to bring them comfort."

When I arrived, the small hospital room was packed with people, all surrounding the bed where this beautiful little girl was lying, lifeless. Everyone was in tears, but I could immediately make out the parents because they were clinging by the bed of their precious child. At first, I just cried with them. In situations like this, *often there are no words—only laments.* We prayed to the Lord together, and I asked God to provide the comfort that he alone can give. We talked briefly about Jesus, about his victory over death—but in that moment it was death that felt closer than anything else.

Deep down inside, I felt an overwhelming sense of helplessness. No platitudes or prayers can take away the sense of loss—the void created through a sudden and premature death like that. I remember longing for Jesus—knowing that I could do nothing—longing for Jesus to come and do something.

If you've ever seen death close up, you may have felt helpless like that too. It's something I think many people were feeling just recently when the whole coronavirus pandemic began to shut things down. The overwhelming sense of not knowing what to do, feeling like they're not in control anymore. So often as a society, we try to cover up death. We avoid the topic and pretend as if it isn't coming; but no matter how hard we try to hide from it, death confronts us. Sometimes slowly, through disease; other times immediately through tragedy. It's in those moments that we're forced to grapple with it.

Death is everyone's problem. It doesn't avoid prominent people and just attack poor communities. The whole world watched in shock when the prime minister of England was put on a ventilator because of the coronavirus. Thankfully, he survived—but others have not been as fortunate. We see desperation all around us. If it isn't a pandemic, it's something else that inevitably reminds of us our mortality.

If you've felt this helplessness, then you can begin to understand how the two people in this portion of Scripture felt. The helplessness of a father, watching his daughter's life slip away; and the helplessness of a woman who has given everything she has to find a cure herself and is at the end of her rope. Two people who in many respects couldn't have been more different but who share a common problem. We also share this problem with them: It's the problem of mortality.

By the way, you don't have to be a Christian to recognize that mortality is a problem—*the* problem—that humanity faces. Atheist historian Yuval Noah Harari clearly made this point in his best-selling book *Homo Deus*. He noted that millions of dollars are being spent by Silicon Valley luminaries, seeking to figure out how to prolong human life and eventually make humans *a-mortal*. That is, you wouldn't die from old age, but you could still die from a car accident or an act of violence. Harari is optimistic that humanity will one day conquer mortality:

> We don't need to wait for the Second Coming in order to overcome death. A couple of geeks in a lab can do it. If traditionally death was the specialty of priests and theologians, now the engineers are taking over.[1]

It seems at least some are mobilizing in the fight against death, investing large sums of money to solve the problem of human helplessness. In Jesus, however, we have a better way, which we see as we look at his interaction with the two helpless people in our passage: a prominent man named Jairus, and a poor and nameless woman.

Jairus was the kind of guy you look up to. From Mark's account, we gather that he was a pillar in his society. He's introduced as a ruler of the synagogue. Now, in case you didn't know, in those days there was a temple in Jerusalem. God had commanded it to be built, and it was there that the priests would offer sacrifices and perform sacred rituals. Besides the temple, though, there were synagogues scattered throughout the world. Synagogues were sort of like teaching hubs for religious instruction. The Torah would be read, psalms would be sung,

---

[1] Yuval Noah Harari, *Homo Deus: A Brief History of Tomorrow* (New York: Harper Perennial, 2018), 26.

and prayers would be prayed.

You can think of a synagogue like you might think of your local church congregation: a body of faithful believers seeking to grow in their understanding of God's Word. In much the same way, Jairus was one of the rulers of the particular synagogue in his area. He was a guy who had it together you might say. Synagogue rulers were in charge of the affairs of the local congregation: the money and the services that were held there. In other words, Jairus has a level or respect and responsibility greater than that of the average person. This is the kind of man you go to when you have a problem or when you need advice.

For all of his prominence, though, Jairus has his own problem. His little girl was at the point of death (v. 23). "She has reached the end," this man tells Jesus. Picture the scene: There's a crowd all around Jesus—men and women following him, talking—and Jairus runs up to Jesus, falling to the ground in front of everyone, begging for help from Jesus. The Greek text suggests that Jairus repeatedly implored Jesus, and you can understand his urgency. "My little girl is about to die, please come Jesus, she's in trouble, heal her, lay your hands on her, *help me!*" Imagine how hard the decision must have been for this man to leave his daughter's side, not knowing which breath will be her last. Would she die when he left the house, before he could reach Jesus? It was probably too difficult for him to consider.

There he is—the prominent, religious leader of the synagogue who has handled his finances well—helpless. So desperate, he leaves his little girl's side and goes searching for Jesus. When Jairus finds Jesus and begs for his help, Jesus agrees to go with him. And, of course, why wouldn't he? Jairus is a *good guy*. I picture Jairus jumping to his feet, grabbing Jesus by the arm and rushing him to his house. Nothing was going to stop Jairus from getting Jesus to his little girl. But something does.

Since the situation couldn't be more urgent, they were both hurrying toward Jairus's home, when all of a sudden there's an interruption. Jesus is stopped. Pulled aside by a woman, another helpless person, but this time someone who wouldn't have been a pillar in that society. In fact, she was considered a pariah.

We don't know her name. We might say that the text depicts her as a nobody. She was someone of zero prominence, not a leader, religious or otherwise—just another needy person. She's known to us only as the woman with the flow of blood. She had been hemorrhaging for twelve years, and we're told in verse 26 that she had "suffered much under many physicians, and had spent all that she had, and was no better but rather grew worse." Like Jairus, she too had heard about Jesus—and she too was at the end of her rope, having tried what seemed like everything but now was bankrupt and ostracized. Her only hope was to touch a portion of Jesus' clothing.

Now, I say she was ostracized because in that day, her condition would have made her ritually *unclean.* Let me explain what I mean by that, because it gives us more insight into her condition. In the Bible, it is revealed that God is the source of life. He has life in himself, and he's not dependent on anyone or anything. When we sin, it's like falling away from life. It tarnishes the very existence we have from God. In the Old Testament, this was vividly portrayed through a system of rituals described in books such as Leviticus. If someone had a disease, or was bleeding in some way, it was a picture of a "loss of life" that would render that person "unclean." It didn't mean they had necessarily done something wrong; it was a sign of how mortality—through sin—has distanced us from God who is the source of life.

As a part of the ancient community, you needed your uncleanness to be dealt with. This is why God gave the people priests and the sacrificial system of worship. If your uncleanness wasn't resolved, *it could spread.* Death and uncleanness were like contagious diseases.

> When a woman has a discharge, and the discharge in her body is blood, she shall be in her menstrual impurity for seven days, and whoever touches her shall be unclean until evening. And everything on which she lies during her impurity shall be unclean. Everything also on which she sits shall be unclean. And whoever touches her bed shall wash his clothes and bathe himself in water and be unclean until evening. . . . If a woman has a discharge of blood for many days, not at the time of her menstrual impurity, or if she has a discharge beyond the time of her impurity, all the days of the discharge she shall continue in her uncleanness.
> (Lev. 15:19–22, 25)

Although these rituals may all sound weird to us, here's what we need to understand: Uncleanness didn't necessarily mean evil, or sin; it meant losing or falling away from life. God is the ultimate life; and if we approach him, then we can't be in a state of lifelessness. Since the state of lifelessness, or uncleanness, was contagious, there were rituals for washing and quarantining. Why? So that you wouldn't spread your uncleanness. You might be able to understand this a little better now as we experience a global pandemic. We understand the importance of hand washing, disinfectant wipes, quarantining, and so on, all to "flatten the curve" and protect people from the spread of the virus. That's very much how the Old Testament ritual system worked.

In this story, we likewise find a woman who should be quarantined. Technically, since whatever she touches becomes unclean, she shouldn't be out in the crowd. But she thinks, "If only I could touch Jesus, maybe I can be made better." She doesn't want anyone to notice her out and about. It would be like someone knowing they had the coronavirus, burning up with a fever and hacking with a cough, running into a crowd of people because they believed the cure was in the crowd. The nameless woman tried to touch Jesus without him knowing.

So here they are: a prominent and well-to-do synagogue leader, respected by the community, and a poor, nameless woman, ostracized and neglected by the community. A pillar of the community in Jairus, and a pariah of the community in the woman who is never named. At this point, I think it's appropriate to make an observation. Humanity might be separated by many things—class, income, race, religion, gender, and so on. Fundamentally, however, we all face the same problem: death. It doesn't matter how prominent you are in society, or how poor you are, one way or another you will be confronted by your mortality. It might be a slow bleed or the sudden onset of illness, but it will hit you with that sense of helplessness, and even hopelessness. It was true for the faithful and religious Jairus, and the poor and nameless woman. They both had—we all have—the same problem.

Actually, there's an interesting way I think this is highlighted in this text. We're told that the woman had this issue of blood for how long? Twelve years. How old is the man's daughter? Twelve years old. It's almost as if, despite everything that separates them—gender, power, prominence, wealth—Jairus and the nameless woman are united by a twelve-year-old problem that only Jesus can fix.

I've heard people who reject God say things like religion is for people who need a crutch; it's for unstable people, weak people. I don't really have a problem with any of that. The problem is that the person who talks like that often assumes they aren't also needy. One of the things this passage shows us is that it doesn't matter who you are—whether you're the most prominent person in your community or the poorest—when it comes to our *ultimate need* for grace and forgiveness, the playing field is level. We *all need Jesus*.

In fact, in the case of Jairus, his inability is put on display in an ironic way. Do you know what Jairus in Hebrew means (according to some lexicons)? "He enlightens" or "he awakens/rouses up." Jairus is the waker-upper! But here's the thing: in the case of his daughter, he is not able to say, "Little girl, rise up." He's the waker who can't do the waking; and while he's frantically leading Jesus to his little girl, they're interrupted and Jesus stops to talk to this poor woman.

How do you handle it when people interrupt you? You're trying to do something, maybe something important, and someone starts tugging on your shoulder—perhaps a child? Imagine Jairus's frustration here. His daughter is on the brink of death, he's trying to rush Jesus to his house, and Jesus stops to talk to this nobody? She touches Jesus, she's healed miraculously, and she begins to recount her story to Jesus there in front of everyone (v. 33). She's sharing about how she's had this problem for twelve years, about the doctors she's gone to, about how no one had helped her, but now she'd been healed (presumably)! If you're Jairus, you're thinking, "Lady, get out of our way!" But Jesus doesn't discard this woman.

Death is not a respecter of persons. It doesn't discriminate against the rich or the poor, the powerful or the weak. You know who else isn't a respecter of persons? Jesus. One of the things we see in Jesus here is that he doesn't pay more attention to this prominent official than he does to the poor and nameless woman. In fact, at least in Mark's Gospel, *this woman is the center of the story,* sandwiched in the story of Jairus. Although we often judge a person's social status, Jesus isn't like that. God, the Creator of the universe, allowed himself to be interrupted by this poor woman. And whereas Jairus is probably stressing, wondering, "Jesus, what about my daughter? She's about to die!" Jesus stops to tend to another daughter. "*Daughter*," Jesus says to this "pariah, "your faith has made you well; go in peace, and be healed of your disease" (v. 34).

As Jesus was saying those precious words to her, someone ran up from Jairus's house and said to him, "Your daughter is dead. Why trouble the teacher any further?" The words that Jairus hoped to hear Jesus speak over his daughter were spoken instead over this disgraced woman. Now it all seemed too late. It's hard to imagine what this man must have felt in that moment. Perhaps he was thinking he should have stayed home to be with his daughter for her final moments. Maybe guilt began to envelop him, no doubt anger, too—anger that this woman, whoever she was, had interrupted them and potentially interfered with his girl's healing. He must have felt devastated until Jesus said to him, "Do not fear, only believe."

At last, they arrived at the house where the mourners were already wailing. In that day, you'd hire professional lamenters to come and mourn for your deceased loved one. Someone who had money and status like Jairus might have more mourners than those with less means. When Jesus said the girl was only sleeping, these mourners laughed. They knew what a dead body looked like. Sending them away, Jesus went into the room with a few of his disciples, the mother, and the father. Taking the little girl by the hand, he then said, "*Talitha cumi*" or "Little girl, arise." What Jairus—the one who awakens—couldn't do, Jesus did. Everyone was amazed.

Most readers of Mark's Gospel miss this, but what Jesus was doing in this story is revealing to us that he's the *ultimate priest*. He's the one who makes us fit to enter into God's presence, who cleanses those who are unclean. In Numbers 5:2, God told Moses,

> "Command the people of Israel that they put out of the camp everyone who is leprous or who has a discharge and everyone who

is unclean through contact with the dead."

Well, in Mark 1:40ff., Jesus touched a leper and cleansed him. Then here with the woman who had this continual discharge of blood, Jesus allowed her to touch him and he cleansed her. Then with Jairus's dead daughter, what did Jesus do? He had contact with the dead, holding her little hand and raising her up. Note here that instead of becoming unclean, Jesus is depicted as this super-priest whose holy presence cleanses the lepers, those with a discharge of blood, and even the dead. It's as if Mark is wanting us to see that in Jesus, we meet the one whose holiness and purity are stronger than all of our uncleanness. Jesus is the contagiously holy priest, and when he touches someone, or is touched by someone, they are cleansed.

By the way, did you know that in the Old Testament, the garments of the high priest were said to transmit holiness? Ezekiel 44:19 says,

> And when they [the priests] go out into the outer court to the people, they shall put off the garments in which they have been ministering and lay them in the holy chambers. And they shall put on other garments, lest they transmit holiness to the people with their garments.

By touching Jesus' robe, the woman was cleansed, and we're given a glimpse into Jesus' identity. He didn't just come to be a wonderworker. He's ultimately the great high priest of God's people, who came to purify all of our uncleanness and to offer up a sacrifice for our sins. He isn't afraid to get his hands dirty with sinners. We're precisely why he came! In this passage, we see that Jesus doesn't discriminate between the pillars or pariahs of society; he came for the helpless. You can't infect Jesus with your sin, but his holy presence can infect you.

You also can experience the cleansing power of Jesus right now. *You can lay hold of Jesus like the woman in this story.* How? You only have to do what she did and what Jesus called Jairus to do: "Only believe." Faith is like a hand, and with it you and I lay hold of Jesus' holy robes. The same Jesus who cured this woman and raised up the little girl is the same Jesus you have access to by believing in him. Do not be afraid; only believe. And that's what the gospel calls everyone to. The prominent and the poor. The Jairuses of the world, and people who feel nameless and neglected. If you haven't laid hold of Jesus, don't let your uncleanness keep you from him. It won't keep you from his love any more than it kept his love from the nameless woman. Be bold in running to him! His holiness is more infectious than your sins; and through his shed blood on the cross and resurrection from the dead, he will do what we can't do for ourselves or for each other—*he* will raise us up!

DISCUSSION QUESTIONS

1. How do you think most people view death in today's society? Is it a problem we need to fight against or a natural part of life we need to embrace?

2. In this story, Jesus ministers to two different people who had nothing in common. Does this give us any insight about how the church should engage in ministry today? Do you think we sometimes focus on one kind of person in the church? What difference does that makes?

3. Many people "touched" Jesus in the crowd, but only the woman was healed. What was different about how she laid hold of Jesus? Do you think it's possible for people today to be "around Jesus" without ever really experiencing his saving power?

4. As our great high priest, what are some of the ways Jesus fulfilled and continues to fulfill his priestly ministry? In this text, he's depicted as the one who deals with the unclean. In what other ways does Jesus act as our high priest?

CHAPTER THREE | *Mark 6:45–52*

The Lord of Creation

DO YOU REMEMBER WHEN YOU LEARNED HOW TO SWIM? There's that moment when you get how do to it and realize it's possible to navigate through the water without help. Although that milestone is exciting, the hard work leading up to learning how to swim isn't as exciting. Actually, it can be quite scary. I was reminded of this when my wife and I purchased swim lessons for our children a couple years back. We'd heard of a particular swim teacher whose crash-course swim class promised to get your toddler pool-safe within a week—in just five short lessons, my kids would be ready for the water!

The guy delivered on his promise, but the first few lessons were pretty intense, especially for our children. Standing beside the pool, my wife and I were instructed not to intervene during the lesson. The instructor would take our kids into the pool (one at a time), and let them loose somewhere in the middle of the water. He'd stand back a foot or two and have them splash their way toward him. Of course, we knew they were safe—but the look on their faces said, "Why are you doing this to me!?" I'll admit, it was hard to watch in the beginning, but by the third lesson, the terror was transformed into excitement and laughter. "Look, I'm swimming!"

I won't ever forget the first two days of swim classes though. Early on, one of our children began confessing all of his sins from the water: "I promise I'll listen to you! I'll always eat my dinner! I won't ever fight with my sister!" He thought we were putting him through some sort of cruel and unusual torture, and he was confused as to why Mom and Dad weren't jumping into the pool to his rescue. Understandably so, he had a hard time seeing our good intentions in the midst of his circumstances.

I think the disciples of Jesus in this Gospel story were suffering from a similar bewilderment. Like my son on his first day of swim lessons, they were splashing around, terrified of drowning, while the one who was supposed to love them watched silently from the shore. Blinded by the wind and waves, when they finally saw Jesus walking toward them, they didn't even recognize him. "It's a ghost!" they thought. Do you ever feel like that? Like you're drowning, and Jesus is just observing from afar? That's where the disciples were in Mark 6.

There are circumstances in life that can cloud your spiritual visibility. Moments where the Son of God becomes distorted, and you view him as cruel instead of compassionate. In this story, the disciples were coming off of a long day of service alongside Jesus. They'd just helped distribute food to the five thousand; and yet, despite their faithful work, Jesus sent them directly into a storm.

Some of the most charitable people in history have had moments—even long seasons—of low spiritual visibility, times where Jesus seemed distant to them. Mother Theresa is respected by many for her selfless service to the people of Calcutta and hailed as a spiritual giant because of her sacrifices. The world was shocked to discover that this woman who seemed so near to God actually questioned his love for much of her life. When many of her private correspondences were published after Theresa's death, they revealed a deep internal struggle:

> Lord, my God, who am I that You should forsake me? The child of your love—and now become as the most hated one—the one You

have thrown away as unwanted—unloved. I call, I cling, I want—and there is no One to answer—no One on whom I can cling. No one. Alone. . . . I am told God loves me—and yet the reality of darkness & coldness & emptiness is so great that nothing touches my soul.[1]

In another place she wrote, "If you only knew what I am going through— He is destroying everything in me."[2] She believed that God was in control of her experience; she just didn't understand why he seemed so distant despite her life of service.

Writing after the death of his wife, C. S. Lewis also spoke about this silent darkness:

> Go to [God] when your need is desperate, when all other help is vain, and what do you find? A door slammed in your face, and a sound of bolting and double bolting inside. After that, silence. . . . Why is he so present a commander in our time of prosperity and so very absent a help in time of trouble?[3]

That's what the disciples had to be wondering. They *knew* Jesus was in control of their situation; after all, he was the one who had sent them out into the water as Mark wrote: "Immediately [Jesus] made his disciples get into the boat and go before him to the other side, to Bethsaida, while he dismissed the crowd" (Mark 6:45). The word Mark used there, *made*, means to strongly urge or compel. This is actually the only time Mark uses it in his Gospel. You get the sense that this is more than a suggestion coming from Jesus. Jesus commanded his disciples into the storm.

---

1 Mother Theresa, *Come Be My Light: The Private Writings of the Saint of Calcutta* (New York: Image, 2007), 187.

2 Mother Theresa, 169

3 C. S., Lewis, *A Grief Observed* (London: Faber & Faber, 1964), 10.

Interestingly, this isn't the first storm in Mark's Gospel. Just back two chapters, the disciples were stuck in the middle of a storm while Jesus slept in the stern (Mark 4:38). On that occasion, the disciples went to Jesus and said, "Teacher, do you not care that we are perishing?" Jesus got up from his nap and rebuked the wind and the sea saying, "Peace! Be still!" The wind and the waters stopped raging, and the disciples trembled wondering, "Who then is this that even the wind and the sea obey him?" (4:41).

The disciples were forced by Jesus to go into the storm, and the disciples knew that Jesus controlled the wind and the waves. They remembered the previous encounter, when Jesus hushed the elements. This time, however, they're in the boat without him.

During those long hours of Christ's absence in the storm, the disciples felt tormented. The Greek word that translates "making headway painfully" (v. 48) is used in the previous chapter of Mark's Gospel when Jesus encountered the demon-possessed man of the Gerasenes. The man fell down and cried out, "What have you to do with me, Jesus, Son of the Most High God? I adjure you by God, do not *torment* me" (Mark 5:7). How ironic that the very thing the demons begged Jesus not to do to them in Mark 5, Jesus seems to do to his disciples in Mark 6 by sending them into the sea. In our suffering, there's the danger that Jesus becomes distorted to us. We can begin to view him as a tormenter, instead of a good savior. Perhaps this is why the disciples thought Jesus was a ghost when he finally showed up. Blinded by their suffering, they had a hard time seeing their savior.

How quickly the disciples forgot the compassion of Jesus, who had just fed a wandering multitude! Jesus wasn't trying to torture his children; rather, he was bringing them closer to himself by revealing his identity to them as the Lord of all creation. This story in particular gives us some helpful direction for those times in our lives when Jesus seems distant.

FIRST, NO MATTER HOW HARD IT IS FOR YOU TO SEE JESUS, HE HAS HIS EYES ON YOU.

Verse 48 says that Jesus *saw* that they were making headway painfully. This is actually quite remarkable. It's dark outside, the weather is stormy, and the disciples are probably two to four miles offshore. They didn't see Jesus—they couldn't! But he was watching them the whole time.

When my wife and I first moved to the neighborhood in Southern California where I planted our church, our house didn't have a washer and dryer. We would take turns going to a local laundromat to do our laundry, usually early in the morning. One weekday, it was my turn to take care of the clothes, and I was going about the routine when an older woman came in to do laundry, followed by three men. The woman had her basket of laundry, but the three men who followed her in weren't carrying anything. She began loading up the washer, anxiously checking over her shoulder. At one point she looked at me and whispered, "Please watch me!" I nodded, smiled, and began speaking to her. The three men lingered for a few minutes and then left. After that experience, I handled all the laundry for our family.

I can still remember her face as she whispered to me, "Please watch me!" She was afraid and simply wanted to know that someone was there to keep an eye on her. She wanted to know she wasn't alone in a potentially dangerous situation. There is a comfort in knowing that someone sees us when we're afraid. That we really *aren't* alone. The disciples may have felt like Jesus had forgotten them, but he hadn't. They might have missed him, distracted by their sinking vessel, but he was watching them. He watches you, too, even when you feel like you're sinking.

That God sees us in the midst of our affliction is demonstrated by the Old Testament story of Hagar. In Genesis 16, Hagar fled from her home, overwhelmed with sorrow. The angel of the Lord appeared to her and promised to multiply her offspring (v. 10), giving her great comfort. Verse 13 says, "She called the name of the Lord who spoke to her, 'You are a God of seeing,' for she said, 'Truly here I have seen him who looks after me.'" A "God of seeing" is the translation of the Hebrew *El-Roi*. The God of the Bible, Jesus, is the God who sees us in our suffering.

SECOND, JESUS IS NEVER JUST IDLY WATCHING YOU; HE'S ACTIVELY PRAYING FOR YOU.

This was Jesus' intent in going up the mountainside to begin with (v. 46). We're not told what Jesus was praying for, but there's good reason to believe that as he was watching his disciples, he was also lifting them up in prayer to the Father. Sadly, many people today don't think of prayer as doing any good. We contrast prayer with action, but prayer *is action*; in fact, it's the most important thing we can do if we want to see any progress in a given situation. Prayer is human action that leads to *divine action*. God has ordained to use the prayers of his people to accomplish his purposes in the world. But even when we fall short of praying, blinded by life's circumstances, Jesus continues to pray for us.

After his resurrection, Jesus ascended to another mountain—the heavenly Mount Zion (Heb. 12:22)—and there he continues to pray for his disciples today. He sees us from heaven and pleads to the Father on our behalf. In the context of describing the sufferings faced by believers, Paul said, "Who is to condemn? Christ Jesus is the one who died—more than that, who was raised—who is at the right hand of God, who indeed is interceding for us" (Rom. 8:34). In Hebrews 7:25, we learn about Jesus' present priestly ministry: "He is able to save to the uttermost those who draw near to God through him, since he always lives to make intercession for them." Did you catch that? *Jesus lives to pray for you.* Not only does he see you, but his prayers also sustain you!

THIRD, IN THE STORMS OF LIFE, JESUS INTENDS TO REVEAL HIMSELF TO YOU.

For years, I was troubled by the second half of Mark 6:48: "About the fourth watch of the night he came to them, walking on the sea. *He meant to pass by them.*" What? The disciples were straining at the oars and Jesus was going to walk right by them? This seems to confirm the human suspicion that God is cruel in our suffering, rubbernecking at our wreckage. The key to this phrase is to understand the Old Testament passages behind it.

> Moses said, "Please show me your glory." And he said, "I will make all my goodness *pass before you* and will proclaim before you my name 'The Lord.' And I will be gracious to whom I will be gracious, and will show mercy on whom I will show mercy. But," he said, "you cannot see my face, for man shall not see me and live." And the Lord said, "Behold, there is a place by me where you shall stand on the rock, and *while my glory passes by* I will put you in a cleft of the rock, and I will cover you with my hand *until I have passed by.* Then I will take away my hand, and you shall see my back, but my face shall not be seen. (Exod. 33:18–23)

> And behold, the word of the Lord came to him, and he said to him, "What are you doing here, Elijah?" He said, "I have been very jealous for the Lord, the God of hosts. For the people of Israel have forsaken your covenant, thrown down your altars, and killed your prophets with the sword, and I, even I only, am left, and they seek

my life, to take it away." And he said, "Go out and stand on the mount before the Lord." *And behold, the Lord passed by*, and a great and strong wind tore the mountains and broke in pieces the rocks before the Lord, but the Lord was not in the wind. And after the wind an earthquake, but the Lord was not in the earthquake. And after the earthquake a fire, but the Lord was not in the fire. And after the fire the sound of a low whisper. (1 Kings 19:9–12)

Who alone stretched out the heavens,
    and *trampled the waves of the sea*;
who made the Bear and Orion,
    the Pleiades and the chambers of the south;
who does great things beyond searching out,
    and marvelous things beyond number.
Behold, he passes by me, and I see him not;
    he moves on, but I do not perceive him. (Job 9:8–11)

In the Old Testament, this language of "passing by" was often used in the context of God's self-revelation. He is the compassionate Lord of Creation who tramples on the waves! When he passes by his people, he's revealing himself to them in a way that our finite minds can grasp. It's a heavenly condescension that reaches its pinnacle in the incarnation of the Son of God, Jesus. When Jesus trampled on the waves before the boat beside the disciples, he was revealing to them that he's the God of Exodus 33, 1 Kings 19, and Job 9; he's the gracious one who is full of mercy and compassion for his people. How tragic that the disciples, so blinded by their circumstances, saw a ghost instead of God!

Can we blame them though? The reality is that we misinterpret our circumstances all the time, too. We begin to question God's love and power when things don't go our way. We assume he's stopped paying attention to us, and we begin to live as if we were no longer under his watchful eye. If the disciples had a hard time *seeing Jesus*, then we shouldn't be surprised when we also have a hard time.

When that happens, dear friend, remember that he sees you and prays for you, and he wants to reveal his love to you—a love most vividly displayed when Jesus climbed up another mountain called Calvary. There, the one who trampled on the waves of the sea was trampled by sinful men. The one who hung the constellations—the Bear and Orion, and the Pleiades—was himself hung on the cross of wood. Behold how gracious and compassionate he is!

DISCUSSION QUESTIONS

1. After a long day of serving, the disciples were sent by Jesus into a tumultuous storm. Do you ever feel like Jesus sends you to places you'd rather not go? If so, how do you respond in those situations?

2. This booklet is all about rightly "seeing" Jesus, but it's obvious from this text that sometimes we have a hard time doing that. When do you have the most difficulty seeing Jesus clearly? How do you deal with those seasons?

3. Do you sometimes think Jesus has forgotten you "in the storm"? Does the reality that Jesus sees you and prays for you bring you comfort?

4. When Jesus was going to "pass by" his disciples, what was he trying to teach them? Do you think Jesus has lessons he's trying to teach us in our suffering? What are some lessons you've learned in the past?

CHAPTER FOUR | *Matthew 21:12–17*

The Zealous Redeemer

IT WAS A BEAUTIFUL DAY IN SOUTHERN CALIFORNIA and hundreds of people were gathered together to celebrate the graduating class of 2019 at San Ysidro High School. The ceremony was run of the mill until class valedictorian, Natalie Buhr, gave her speech. It began like most graduation speeches: she thanked her friends and family, together with a handful of teachers, and then the tenor of her speech shifted, which caused her to receive nationwide attention.

> To my counselor, thank you for letting me fend for myself—you were always unavailable; . . . you had absolutely no role in my achievements. . . . To the main office, your negligence to inform me of several scholarships until the day before they were due potentially caused me to miss out on thousands of dollars. To the teacher that was regularly intoxicated during class this year, thank you for using yourself to teach these students about the dangers of alcoholism.[1]

The audience gasped and at various points even broke into applause. Many of them agreed with Natalie's assessment, feeling the administration had failed the students in several ways. Others thought Natalie's actions were too dramatic and that she was condemning the whole school because of a few bad apples. As you could imagine, her actions were polarizing—some cheered, while others were indignant and embarrassed.

---

1   https://965tic.radio.com/articles/watch-high-school-valedictorian-scorch-faculty-graduation-speech.

Whether or not you agree with her approach, she was attempting to turn the tables over on what she believed was an incompetent system. The truth is, even organizations that are supposed to provide helpful services can become corrupt. We may not all agree on which organizations are most in need of this table-turning ceremony, but we know they're out there!

The shocking thing about Matthew 21:12–17 is *where* the tables are being turned over, and *who* is causing the scene. Jesus, the one we've already identified as the Lord of all Creation, is turning over the tables in his Father's house, the temple! Jesus isn't at the local tavern, cleansing Jerusalem's bars. He has not gone to the office of the tax collectors. That would have made sense, since tax collectors were viewed as traitors to the Jewish nation, and they would engage in corrupt practices to make extra money. But Jesus wasn't flipping over the tax tables. He didn't even go to the local brothel to decry the sexual immorality of that society (although we know that Jesus stood firmly against it). Instead, Jesus went to the one place where we didn't expect a problem—God's house—and he starts turning the place upside down.

When Matthew says that Jesus entered the temple and *drove out* all who sold and bought in the temple, the term "drive out" is the same word he used to describe Jesus driving demons out of people (See Matt. 8:16; 9:33; 10:1; 12:28). It's as if Jesus is performing a temple exorcism, casting out the sin hidden behind the sacred walls.

Some years ago, police in Boston arrested the fifty-seven-year-old pastor of Mission Church, a church that housed a 12-step recovery program for substance abuse. An investigation discovered that the church was actually a front for an illegal drug operation. Police found crack cocaine, fentanyl, Percocet, pills, and $10,000 in drug money inside the building. The surrounding community was shocked and some wondered how the pastor—who seemed like such a nice guy!—could be involved in such a thing.

This passage in Matthew is meant to create that kind of shock in you. *The temple is being turned upside down by God himself.* The institution that's supposed to be the safest—the most solid—is exposed as sinister. In fact, Jesus called it a den of thieves (v. 13)!

It's easy to see the corruption all around us. The incompetence and even abuse of power in business, or Hollywood, or the government. We can point it out, and we may even have solutions in our minds for how to make things better in the world. Our challenge, however, is with recognizing the reformation that the church needs. But sometimes the most difficult corruption to see *is the corruption that exists in our own hearts.* Although Jesus will one day cleanse the whole world, he begins by cleansing the church—his people—to make us fit worshipers of the Triune God (see 1 Pet. 4:17).

In verse 13, Jesus quotes from Isaiah 56 and Jeremiah 7. In the Jeremiah reference, Jeremiah was told by God to go and proclaim a message at the doorway of the temple as people were going in to worship. Try and picture worshipers walking into the temple (sort of like they were doing on the day Jesus turned the tables over) as Jeremiah stood at the doorway shouting:

> Amend your ways and your deeds, and I will let you dwell in this place. Do not trust in these deceptive words: 'This is the temple of the Lord, the temple of the Lord, the temple of the Lord.' For if you truly amend your ways and your deeds, if you truly execute justice one with another, if you do not oppress the sojourner, the fatherless, or the widow, or shed innocent blood in this place, and if you do not go after other gods to your own harm, then

I will let you dwell in this place, in the land that I gave of old to your fathers forever. Behold, you trust in deceptive words to no avail. Will you steal, murder, commit adultery, swear falsely, make offerings to Baal, and go after others gods that you have not known, and then come and stand before me in this house, which is called by my name, and say, 'We are delivered!'—only to go on doing all these abominations? Has this house, which is called by my name, become a den of robbers in your eyes? (Jer. 7:3–11)

The people in Jeremiah's day were going through the motions of worship, all the while clinging to their sins. Their confidence was in external rituals, finding security in their religious observance, while not truly trusting in Yahweh. Ironically, by putting a stop to their worship on that day, Jesus revealed to us some important principles regarding how God wants to be worshiped.

FIRST, THE BUILDING IS NOT THE SOURCE OF THE BLESSING.

You might have seen the news footage from when the famous Cathedral of Notre Dame caught fire. One of the most beautiful pieces of architecture in the world, considered by many to be a holy place—a cathedral—and yet the whole thing was in flames during Holy Week in 2019. This "holy place" was on fire during a "holy time" while millions watched in shock from their television or computer screens.

When Jesus marched into Jerusalem and cleansed the temple, he did it during a time that was for many Jews similar to our holy week: the Passover. His actions would have been unsettling to those who put their hope in the temple rituals. Christ knew it wasn't the temple that blessed them, but the *God who lived in the temple.*

What is it that makes a church a sacred place? It isn't the ornate architecture or the crosses that may decorate the walls. It's not the stained glass or the pews. Church happens when the people of God are gathered together under the ministry of the Word to receive the sacraments of grace—baptism and the Lord's Supper. That can happen in a cathedral or on a grass field. What makes God present isn't the wallpaper but the Word!

There are churches that meet in beautiful spaces, but they are dead because the gospel isn't being preached in them. We have to be careful that we don't fall into the trap that the people long ago fell into—putting our confidence in ritual without faith. Buildings can burn down, but the Word of the Lord endures forever. This truth was especially important for the people in Jesus' day to grasp, because in just a short while the temple would be demolished by the Roman army. If their hope remained in the Jerusalem temple, it would be completely shattered by AD 70.

SECOND, RITUAL WITHOUT REPENTANCE CANNOT SAVE YOU.

In Jeremiah's day and in Jesus' day, the people wanted ritual instead of repentance. They brought their sacrifices to the temple, going through the motions of worship, but they continued to follow after their own sinful inclinations. This doesn't mean that ritual is bad. There are biblical rituals that God calls us to observe in worship like baptism and Holy Communion. But observing those rituals without repentance and faith is dangerous.

In the Old Testament, when King David sinned against the Lord by taking

Bathsheba for himself and murdering her husband, he knew there was nothing he could do to win back God's favor.

> For you will not delight in sacrifice, or I would give it;
> you will not be pleased with burnt offering.
> The sacrifices of God are a broken spirit;
> a broken and contrite heart, O God, you will not despise.
> (Ps. 51:16–17)

It wasn't that sacrifice was bad—God has instituted it!—but ritual is never meant to be severed from repentance and faith.

THIRD, GOD SEES BENEATH THE SURFACE OF OUR HYPOCRISY.

I want you to imagine for a moment that you personally are a temple of God. The Bible, of course, uses this language. Paul said that if we belong to Jesus, then we are temples of the Holy Spirit (1 Cor. 6:19). If Jesus showed up today in your temple, would he flip over some tables?

Many of us can look good on the outside, but we know that the external front we put up is just a cover. That's actually how the temple in Jerusalem was during the days of Jesus. On the outside it looked beautiful, but within it was a den of robbers. The first-century historian Josephus helps us imagine the glory of the Jerusalem temple:

> Now the outward face of the temple in its front wanted nothing that was likely to surprise either men's minds, or their eyes. For it was covered all over with plates of gold, of great weight: and at the first rising of the sun reflected back a very fiery splendor, and made those who forced themselves to look upon

it, to turn their eyes away: just as they would have done at the sun's own rays. But this temple appeared to strangers, when they were coming to it at a distance, like a mountain covered with snow. For as to those parts of it that were not gilt, they were exceeding white.[2]

The temple was built from white bricks and covered all over with gold and silver. In the sunlight, it looked like it was glowing, but inside, it was dark.

I wonder if sometimes we aren't too different from that temple. On the outside, everything looks good. Others might say we glow with God's presence. We're adorned with all sorts of gifts, and we bolster our image so that, at least before others, we look pretty glorious. Inside, however, it's a different story. Our lives are actually a mess, and our hearts are captive to sin. Yes, we can go through the motions, but we know that deep down inside, there's no peace. We know that what others see and what God sees are two different things.

This is a tragic and exhausting way to live. It's a twenty-four-hour-a-day job pretending to be something you're not, and many people end up collapsing under the burden. Thankfully, if you're tired of that kind of religion and in need of redemption, Jesus is a zealous redeemer. He knows that for each of us, there are still areas in the temple of our hearts that need cleansing—areas we might be blind to but that he sees. As the zealous redeemer, Jesus stands against all of our religious hypocrisy; he wants to cleanse us of it.

---

2 "The Wars of the Jews or History of the Destruction of Jerusalem," *The Works of Josephus*, ed. and trans. William Whiston (Peabody, MA: Hendrickson, 1987), 5.222.

LASTLY, YOU DON'T HAVE TO BE A THEOLOGIAN OR PRIEST TO WORSHIP GOD HOW HE WANTS TO BE WORSHIPED: IN SINCERITY.

Actually, in this Gospel passage, it was the chief priests and scribes who completely missed out on true worship! How can you worship God the way he wants? According to this text in Matthew, you need to recognize that you're *lame*. After Jesus kicked out all the money changers, those who bought and sold, who then did he receive? "And the blind and the lame came to him in the temple, and he healed them" (v. 14).

The crowds who came in with their own offerings, seeking to justify themselves through their religious observance, were removed from the temple courts. Instead of them, Jesus welcomed those who had *nothing*. Note this: Those who seek to justify themselves with their own offerings in hand are cast out, and those who have nothing to contribute are welcomed in. This is what makes the gospel such good news. It isn't an exchange: your religious obedience for Jesus' love and forgiveness. It's Jesus lavishing his love and forgiveness on people who are lame, on sinners who come to him empty-handed.

This glorious scene caused a group of small children nearby to cry out, "Hosanna to the Son of David!" (v. 15) When the religious leaders took offense at this, Jesus responded by quoting from Psalm 8, "Out of the mouths of infants and nursing babies you have prepared praise." True worshipers come to God like little children, with nothing to contribute, but with faith to receive. Although you may not understand all the deep mysteries of theology, like these children you can also say, "Hosanna to the Son of David!"

Hosanna is the Greek form of a Hebrew word that means "save us." When they cried out "Hosanna!" the children saw Jesus for who he really was, the *savior*. When they referred to him as the Son of David, they recognized him as the true king and ruler over God's people. In worship, we come before God humbly and recognize Jesus as our savior *and* king. What the scribes missed the children saw. Jesus prayed earlier in Matthew 11:25, "I thank you, Father, Lord of heaven and earth, that you have hidden these things from the wise and understanding and revealed them to little children." The gospel remains hidden to the self-righteous, eluding them because they don't think they need it. But for the helpless, the lame, the children who have nothing to contribute, it's the best news in the world.

Do you recognize your need for the gospel, or have you been hiding behind the golden walls of self-righteousness? Pray for the zealous redeemer to do his cleansing work, and see Jesus as the one who confronts all false religion and hypocritical worship. He calls us to recognize him as savior (Hosanna!) and king (the Son of David)—to understand that he is the substance of all true religion.

Matthew mentions something interesting here that I think we often miss: Jesus put a stop to both those who were selling in the temple *and those who were buying* (v.12). In other words, it wasn't just the corrupt salespeople, but the people who were looking to purchase a sacrifice for their worship that day. Why would Jesus put a stop to something that God seemed to have commanded in the Old Testament? Because Jesus was the fulfillment of everything the Old Testament foreshadowed! Jesus put a halt to the buyers because he was *the Lamb of God who would take away the sin of the world* (John 1:29). Those offerings always pointed to him; and through his sacrificial death, they would be brought to an end. By stopping the sacrifices at that moment, Jesus was preparing the world for what he was about to do: put a halt to those sacrifices for all time through his once-for-all sacrifice (Heb. 10:14).

When Jesus turned the tables upside down in Jerusalem, he gave us a far better table. One where we wouldn't have to purchase sacrificial offerings to bring to God, but where we could *receive freely* the once-for-all offering he made for us. It's a gift. Jesus reformed worship and put himself at the center, and he made us the recipients of his boundless love. Every time you go to church to hear God's Word preached and to receive Communion at the Lord's Table, you are benefiting from the worship our zealous redeemer instituted. You don't have to bring a sacrifice, because his was sufficient and through it our sinful hearts are cleansed. What's left, then, for us to do?

> Let us draw near with a sincere heart in full assurance of faith, with our hearts sprinkled clean from an evil conscience and our bodies washed with pure water. Let us hold fast the confession of our hope without wavering, for he who promised is faithful. And let us consider how to stir up one another to love and good works, not neglecting to meet together, as is the habit of some, but encouraging one another, and all the more as you see the Day drawing near. (Heb. 10:22–25)

DISCUSSION QUESTIONS

1. Do you think that, sometimes in the church, we focus so much on the sins of society that we neglect to do our own "housecleaning," so to speak?

2. Jesus clearly cares about right worship. Do you think the church today has minimized or forgotten this aspect of Jesus' teaching? Why or why not?

3. It seems that we are called to be childlike in approaching God in worship, and yet at the same time to pursue truth and a mature understanding of the Word. How do we pursue biblical knowledge while remaining humble and aware of our own sinfulness?

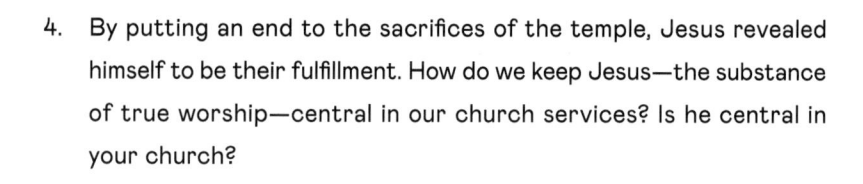

4. By putting an end to the sacrifices of the temple, Jesus revealed himself to be their fulfillment. How do we keep Jesus—the substance of true worship—central in our church services? Is he central in your church?

Made in the USA
Middletown, DE
20 February 2025